Alligators

by Grace Hansen

ABDO
REPTILES
Kids

Visit us at www.abdopublishing.com

Published by Abdo Kids, a division of ABDO, P.O. Box 398166, Minneapolis, Minnesota 55439.

Copyright © 2015 by Abdo Consulting Group, Inc. International copyrights reserved in all countries. No part of this book may be reproduced in any form without written permission from the publisher.

Printed in the United States of America, North Mankato, Minnesota.

032014

092014

 PRINTED ON RECYCLED PAPER

Photo Credits: Getty Images, iStock, Shutterstock, Thinkstock

Production Contributors: Teddy Borth, Jennie Forsberg, Grace Hansen

Design Contributors: Dorothy Toth, Renée LaViolette, Laura Rask

Library of Congress Control Number: 2013952079

Cataloging-in-Publication Data

Hansen, Grace.

 Alligators / Grace Hansen.

  p. cm. -- (Reptiles)

ISBN 978-1-62970-057-1 (lib. bdg.)

Includes bibliographical references and index.

1. Alligators--Juvenile literature.   I. Title.

597.98--dc23

2013952079

Table of Contents

Alligators

Alligators are reptiles.

All reptiles have **scales**
and are **cold-blooded**.

4

Alligators live in Southeastern United States and China. Freshwater ponds and **wetlands** are good places to find alligators.

Alligators have very thick skin. Their skin can be brown or black. They have black stripes on their tails.

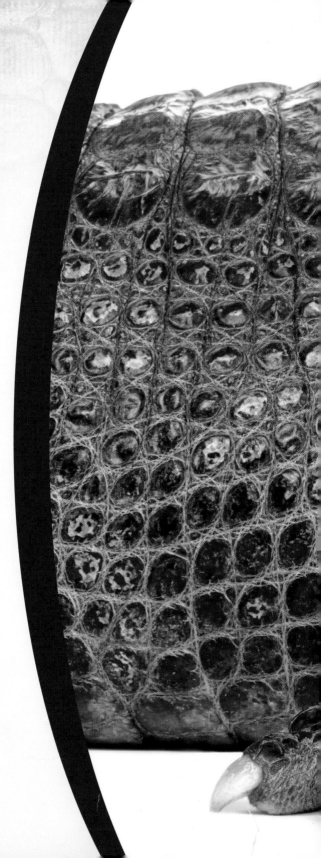

9

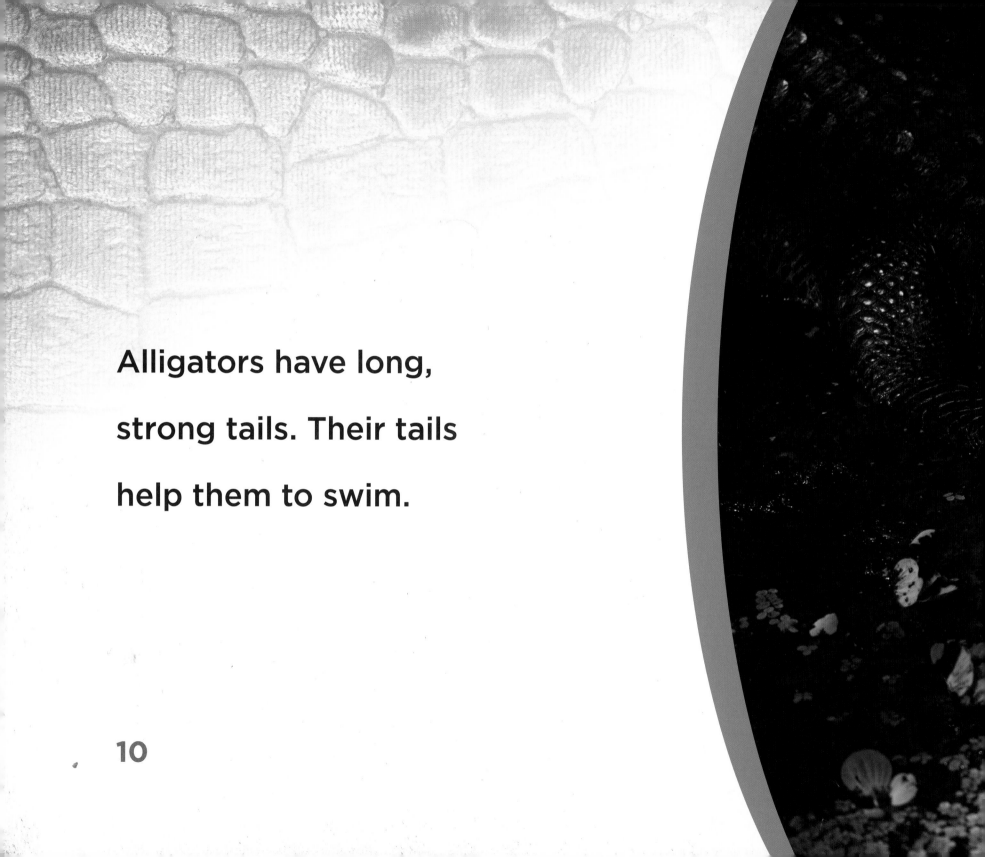

Alligators have long,
strong tails. Their tails
help them to swim.

10

11

Alligators have **webbed** feet.

Their feet help them to swim and walk through mud.

Alligators can swim fast.

They can run quickly for

a short amount of time.

14

Food

Alligators like to eat birds and fish. They also eat big and small **mammals**.

Baby Alligators

A female alligator uses mud, leaves, and twigs to make a **nest**. She lays her eggs in the nest.

Baby alligators **hatch** from the eggs in about 60 days. They stay with their mothers for about two years.

21

More Facts

- Alligators are sometimes said to be "living fossils." That is because they have been around for millions of years.

- Alligators have a powerful jaw to bite down. But their jaw muscles to open their mouths are weak. Humans can hold an alligator's mouth shut with their hands.

- A mother alligator will carry her babies to the water in her mouth after they **hatch**.

Glossary

cold-blooded – animals whose blood temperature depends on the temperature outside.

hatch – to be born from an egg.

mammal – a warm-blooded animal that has hair and whose females produce milk to feed their young.

nest – a place where animals lay their eggs.

scales – flat plates that form the outer covering of reptiles.

webbed – having toes that are joined together with skin.

wetlands – land mostly covered by water.

Index

abdokids.com

Use this code to log on to abdokids.com and access crafts, games, videos and more!

Abdo Kids Code:
RAK0571